Breath, Balance, Believe

A Woman's Blueprint for Stress Relief, Mind Reset, and Body Rejuvenation

Elsie James

Table of Contents

Introduction

In today's fast-paced society, it's easy to feel overwhelmed and out of balance. Consider Susan, a lady in her mid-forties who must balance job, family, and everyday chores. Despite her apparent success, Susan struggles with stress and worry on a daily basis. If this sounds similar, you aren't alone. But what if I told you there's a practical guide—a roadmap, if you will—that might take you to a more relaxed, balanced, and active life? Here comes **"Breath, Balance, Believe:** *A Woman's Blueprint for Stress Relief, Mind Reset, and Body Rejuvenation."*

In this eye opening book, I explore the complexities of regaining our well-being one breath at a time. Drawing on cutting-edge research in psychology, neurology, and holistic health, I provide practical ways for achieving balance and harmony in the midst of life's complications.

I investigate the effectiveness of breathwork, mindfulness, movement, and self-care in promoting our mental, emotional, and physical well-being using a combination of ancient knowledge and modern research.

However, this book goes beyond theory and provides tangible strategies that you may implement in your daily life to experience substantial changes in your well-being. Whether you want to relieve chronic stress, build resilience and inner peace, or just reconnect with your body and soul, *"Breath, Balance, Believe"* gives a road map for navigating the challenges of modern life with grace, fortitude, and vitality.

As you read these pages, I encourage you to have an open heart and mind to the opportunities that await you. Release the limiting ideas that are holding you back and embrace your limitless potential inside. With each turn of the page, may you gain new insights, awaken hidden strengths, and embark on a journey toward a life of pleasure, contentment, and well-being.

So, are you ready to breathe deeply, discover balance, and accept belief? Join me as we begin on this adventure together. Your beautiful, robust self awaits. Let us take the first step forward.

Part I: Understanding Stress

Stress is an apparently ubiquitous companion in the modern world, affecting people of all ages, genders, and socioeconomic backgrounds. However, for women, stress presents particular problems and repercussions that can have a significant influence on their health and well-being.

CHAPTER 1

Unmasking Stress: The Impact On Women's Health

Stress is the body's natural reaction to perceived dangers or difficulties. When confronted with a stressor, such as a looming deadline, a demanding work, financial difficulties, event interpersonal issues, the body's stress response mechanism, known as the fight-or-flight response, kicks in.

This causes a series of physiological changes, including the production of stress hormones like cortisol and adrenaline, an increase in heart rate, heightened attention, and muscular tensing.

In the short term, this response can be adaptive, allowing us to react rapidly to danger and negotiate difficult situations more efficiently.

However, prolonged or excessive stress can have a negative impact on both our physical and mental health.

Chronic stress has been related to a wide range of health problems, including cardiovascular disease, hypertension, obesity, diabetes, impaired immunological function, gastrointestinal disorders, and reproductive concerns.

Furthermore, the consequences of stress are not restricted to the body; they can emerge as psychological symptoms such as anxiety, sadness, irritability, mood swings, and cognitive impairment.

The Gendered Experience Of Stress

While stress affects people of both genders, research indicates that women may be more prone to its effects owing to a combination of biological, psychological, and sociocultural variables.

Women's stress sensitivity and reactivity can be influenced by hormonal variations, especially during menstruation, pregnancy, and menopause.

Furthermore, women's increased frequency of illnesses including autoimmune disorders and chronic pain syndromes may increase their vulnerability to stress-related health issues.

Psychologically, women are frequently conditioned to prioritize caregiving and nurturing duties, putting additional strain on them to combine job, family, and personal obligations.

The *"superwoman syndrome"* - the assumption that women must achieve in numerous domains at the same time - can lead to feelings of inadequacy, shame, and fatigue when these expectations are unrealistic.

Furthermore, cultural norms and preconceptions about femininity and masculinity may influence women's coping mechanisms and emotional expression, affecting how they perceive and respond to stresses.

Hidden Costs of Stress on Women's Health

While the physical indications of stress are typically more visible, the influence on women's mental and emotional well-being is just as important.

According to studies, women are more prone than males to suffer from stress-related mental health problems such as anxiety and depression, with a disproportionate number of women seeking diagnosis and treatment.

Furthermore, the interconnectedness of gender with other social identities such as race, ethnicity, sexual orientation, and socioeconomic position might amplify the impacts of stress and contribute to health inequalities among women.

One especially troubling aspect of chronic stress is its effect on reproductive health. Stress has been linked to menstruation irregularities, infertility, pregnancy problems, premature delivery, and postpartum depression, demonstrating the complex connection between the mind and body.

In addition, the stress of caring for children, elderly parents, or loved ones with chronic diseases can have a negative impact on women's health, often jeopardizing their own self-care and well-being.

"Stress is more than a transient mood or nuisance; it is a complicated physiological reaction that affects all aspects of our being, from our thoughts and feelings to our physical health and well-being."

CHAPTER 2

The Science of Stress: How It Affects Your Mind and Body

The autonomic nervous system (ANS), a complex network of neurons and neurotransmitters that governs involuntary biological activities such as heart rate, digestion, and breathing, is central to our body's stress response. Within the ANS, the sympathetic nervous system (SNS) and the parasympathetic nervous system (PNS) collaborate to maintain a delicate balance of arousal and relaxation.

When we meet a stressor, such as a physical threat, emotional difficulty, event imagined danger, the SNS is activated, initiating the body's fight-or-flight response. This triggers a series of physiological changes that prepare us to confront or flee the threat. The heart rate raises, blood pressure rises, muscles strain, and the body produces stress chemicals like cortisol and adrenaline, ready us for action.

While this reaction is necessary for survival in acute, life-threatening events, chronic or extended activation of the stress response can have a negative impact on our health. Over time, frequent exposure to stress hormones can disturb the body's delicate equilibrium, resulting in a variety of physical and psychological problems.

Impact on the Brain

Stress has a significant impact on the brain, which is the control center of our neurological system. In reaction to stress, the brain goes through a sequence of changes that affect our thoughts, feelings, and behaviors. The amygdala is the brain's emotional center and plays an important part in the processing of fear and stress.

When the amygdala recognizes a threat, it instructs the hypothalamus to release stress chemicals from the adrenal glands. These chemicals, notably cortisol and adrenaline, flood the brain and body, mobilizing resources for action while increasing our senses and awareness.

Simultaneously, prolonged stress impairs the prefrontal cortex, the brain's executive control region in charge of decision-making, problem solving, and emotional regulation. This can hamper our capacity to think clearly, make informed decisions, and deal effectively with situations, resulting in feelings of overload, anxiety, and powerlessness.

Physiological Effects on the Body

Aside from the brain, stress has a significant influence on almost every system in the body, including the cardiovascular and respiratory systems, the immunological and digestive systems. When the stress response is initiated, blood flow is shifted away from non-essential activities like digestion and immunity and toward crucial organs and muscles that are required for life.

As a result, digestion may lag, causing symptoms including indigestion, bloating, and constipation. Immune function may be reduced, increasing vulnerability to infections and diseases. Muscles can become tight and weary, resulting in stiffness, aches, and discomfort. Furthermore, chronic stress has been related to a higher risk of cardiovascular disease, hypertension, diabetes, obesity, and other chronic health problems.

The Mind-Body Connection

Perhaps most noticeable is the complex interplay between the mind and body during the stress reaction. New study indicates that psychological variables such as stress, worry, and depression can impact the onset and course of medical illnesses, while physical illnesses can increase psychological symptoms.

Individuals with chronic diseases, such as chronic pain, autoimmune disorders, or cancer, may feel increased stress as they deal with the physical and mental consequences of their illness.

Chronic stress, on the other hand, has been proven to intensify chronic pain symptoms, increase inflammation, and decrease immunological function, resulting in a vicious cycle of physical and psychological suffering.

Despite the widespread effects of stress on the mind and body, there is hope. Understanding the science of stress and its consequences enables us to take proactive efforts to reduce our stress levels and increase our health and well-being.

"Stress is an unavoidable aspect of life, but not all stresses are created equal. While some obstacles are easily overcome, others can set off a chain reaction of physical and emotional responses, leaving us feeling overwhelmed, tired, and out of control."

CHAPTER 3

Identifying Your Stress Triggers: Finding Balance Starts Here

In our modern society, it's common to become immersed in the busy routines of daily life without pausing to acknowledge the impact that stress may have on our health and well-being. However, becoming aware is the first step toward making a change.

By tuning into your thoughts, feelings, and physiological sensations, you may begin to identify the hidden sources of stress in your life and acquire clarity on what is actually important to you.

External vs Internal Stressors

Stressors take many different forms, ranging from external events and situations to interior ideas, beliefs, and emotions. External stresses might include work deadlines, financial demands, interpersonal difficulties, or big life transitions like moving, beginning a new career, or losing a loved one. Internal pressures, on the other hand, might arise from negative self-talk, perfectionism, self-doubt, or unreasonable expectations.

Common Stress Triggers for Women

While stress may be caused by a variety of circumstances, women may be more prone to certain stresses owing to societal expectations, gender roles, and cultural norms. For example, women are frequently expected to manage several tasks and obligations, such as caring, housework, and job goals, putting them at risk of stress and exhaustion.

More so, women may experience particular stresses associated with reproductive health, such as pregnancy, delivery, and menopause, which can worsen hormone imbalances and emotional discomfort.

Identifying Personal Stress Triggers

To start identifying your specific stress triggers, keep a stress notebook or diary and write down any circumstances, activities, or interactions that make you feel tense, nervous, or overwhelmed. Pay close attention to repeated patterns and themes, as well as any physical or emotional signs that indicate the presence of stress. Are there any persons, locations, or activities that consistently elicit your stress response? Are there certain moments of the day or week when you feel more anxious than usual?

Gathering this information allows you to begin to discover the common threads that underpin your stress and build more effective stress management practices.

Understanding the Effects of Stress on Your Wellbeing

Once you've recognized your stressors, you should think about how they're affecting your general health and wellbeing. Are there any aspects of your life, such as job, relationships, or health, that are disproportionately affected by stress? What physical, mental, and emotional effects does stress have on you?

Common physical stress symptoms include headaches, muscular tension, exhaustion, digestive problems, and sleep difficulties, while psychological symptoms include impatience, mood swings, anxiety, and trouble focusing.

Strategies to Manage Stress Triggers

With this information, you can begin to create tailored methods for reducing stress triggers and restoring balance in your life. This may entail establishing boundaries and declining activities or commitments that deplete your energy, prioritizing self-care techniques such as exercise, meditation, and enjoyable hobbies, and seeking help from friends, family, or professional services like as therapy or counseling.

It might also include reframing negative attitudes and beliefs, practicing self-compassion and acceptance, and developing resilience in the face of hardship.

These strategies will be discussed in details in the subsequent chapters.

Part II: Breath: Techniques for Inner Calm

"Amidst the rapid pace of contemporary living, we often overlook the significance of our breath, treating it as a mere automatic bodily function. Yet, beneath the surface lies a profound source of healing, resilience, and transformation – the power of breath."

CHAPTER 4

The Power of Breath: Harnessing Breathwork for Stress Relief

Breathwork is defined as the intentional and conscious manipulation of the breath to attain certain physical, mental, and emotional results. From the regular rise and fall of our chest to the delicate expansion and contraction of our diaphragm, each breath has the power to control our nervous system, balance our emotions, and harmonize our body and mind.

From a physiological standpoint, the breath is inextricably related to the autonomic nervous system (ANS), a component of the nervous system that regulates involuntary biological activities including heart rate, digestion, and breathing.

By changing the rate, depth, and pattern of our breath, we can directly influence the activity of the sympathetic nervous system (SNS), which is responsible for the body's fight-or-flight response, and activate the parasympathetic nervous system (PNS), which is responsible for the body's rest-and-digest response.

Techniques for Breathing Awareness

Breath awareness is a simple but effective breathwork method that involves paying conscious attention to the natural pattern of the breath as it travels in and out of the body. Observing the breath without judgment or interference can help us develop a sense of presence, awareness, and inner tranquility.

To begin, select a comfortable sitting posture, close your eyes, and breathe deeply to center yourself. Allow your breath to return to its normal rate and rhythm, noticing the sensations of each inhale and exhale as they emerge and pass.

Consider the gradual rise and fall of your chest, the coldness of the air entering your nose, and the warmth as it escapes. If your mind wanders, gently return your focus to the breath to ground yourself in the present now.

Diaphragmatic Breathing

Another effective breathwork technique is diaphragmatic breathing, commonly known as belly breathing or abdominal breathing.

This technique uses the diaphragm, a huge dome-shaped muscle at the base of the lungs, to suck air down into the lower lobes, filling them with new oxygen and activating the body's relaxation response.

To practice diaphragmatic breathing, place one hand on your chest and the other on your belly. Take a slow, deep breath in through your nose, feeling your belly rise as you fill your lungs with air. Then, slowly and totally exhale through your mouth, allowing your abdomen to gently descend as you release the air. Repeat the technique many times, allowing each breath to slow, deepen, and relax.

Box Breathing

Box breathing, also known as square breathing or four-square breathing, is a simple yet efficient breathwork method for immediately calming the mind and relaxing the nervous system.

To practice box breathing, visualize drawing a square with your breath, inhaling for four counts, holding the breath for four counts, expelling for four counts, and holding the breath out for four counts. Repeat this rhythm numerous times until each breath feels smooth, even, and effortless.

As you breathe, envision the four sides of the square - inhale, hold, exhale, hold - and notice how each breath brings you closer to being centered, grounded, and present.

Alternate Nostril Breathing

Alternate nostril breathing, also known as Nadi Shodhana or Anulom Vilom, is a traditional yogic breathwork practice that balances the flow of energy in the body, calms the mind, and promotes inner harmony and balance.

To practice alternate nostril breathing, take a comfortable sitting position with your spine erect and shoulders relaxed. Close your right nostril with your right thumb, then inhale deeply through your left nostril for four counts. Close your left nostril with your right ring finger, then exhale slowly and thoroughly through your right nostril for four counts. Inhale deeply via your right nostril, then close it with your right thumb and breathe out through your left nostril.

Continue this process, swapping nostrils with each breath, for several rounds, until your breathing becomes smooth, steady, and effortless.

The Advantages of Breathwork for Stress Relief

The advantages of breathwork for stress alleviation are extensive and diverse, spanning physical, mental, and emotional well-being. By actively controlling our breathing, you will trigger the body's relaxation response, reduce stress hormone levels like cortisol and adrenaline, and promote overall calm and relaxation.

Furthermore, breathwork can assist to quiet the mind, minimize racing thoughts and mental clutter, and foster a sense of inner calm and clarity.

Emotionally, breathwork can aid with mood regulation, emotional balance, and the promotion of resilience and serenity in the face of life's obstacles.

Integrating Breathwork Into Your Daily Life

To get the most out of breathwork, make it a regular part of your daily routine. This may entail devoting time each day to formal breathwork exercises, such as those described above, as well as bringing breath awareness into ordinary tasks like walking, driving, or washing dishes.

You may also use breathwork to manage stress in real time, by practicing deep breathing methods whenever you feel overwhelmed, apprehensive, or stiff. With persistent practice and patience, you can use the power of breathing to change your relationship with stress, build resilience, and nurture a deeper feeling of calm and well-being in your life.

"Everyone of us possesses the intrinsic ability to build a sense of serenity, clarity, and inner peace via the practice of mindful meditation."

CHAPTER 5

Mindful Meditation: Cultivating Presence and Peace

Mindfulness is essentially the discipline of paying attention to the present moment with openness, curiosity, and acceptance. Rather than concentrating on the past or worrying about the future, mindfulness encourages us to completely connect with whatever is happening in the present moment, whether it's the sensations of our breath, the sounds of nature, or the ideas and emotions that arise in our minds.

By cultivating a nonjudgmental awareness of our thoughts, feelings, and body sensations, we may gain increased clarity, insight, and compassion, as well as regain our innate ability for presence and calm.

The Practice of Mindful Meditation

Mindful meditation is a disciplined practice that promotes mindfulness via focused attention and awareness.

Typically, we sit quietly in a comfortable posture, close our eyes or soften our focus, and devote our attention to a specific object of meditation, such as the breath, a mantra, or bodily sensations.

As ideas, emotions, and sensations occur, we just watch them with inquiry and kindness, allowing them to pass without being preoccupied with their tale or significance.

When the mind wanders, as it always does, we gently redirect our focus back to the selected object of meditation, anchoring ourselves in the present now.

Breath Awareness Meditation

Breath awareness meditation is one of the most basic and accessible kinds of mindfulness meditation. To practice breath awareness meditation, locate a peaceful spot to sit and close your eyes.

Begin by focusing your attention on the natural rhythm of your breath as it moves in and out of your body. Consider the feelings of each inhale and exhale: the rise and fall of your chest, the coldness of the air as it enters your nose, and the warmth as it leaves. When your mind wanders, gently bring your focus back to the breath, which serves as an anchor to the present moment.

Body Scan Meditation

Body scan meditation is another effective mindfulness technique that entails carefully bringing awareness to every area of the body, from head to toe.

To practice body scan meditation, lie down in a comfortable posture with your eyes closed and your arms by your sides. Begin by focusing your attention on the feelings in your toes, noting any stiffness, pain, or warmth. Move your attention gradually up through the body, focusing on the feet, ankles, calves, knees, thighs, hips, belly, chest, shoulders, arms, hands, neck, and head. Pause to examine any sensations that occur without judgment or resistance.

As you scan each region of your body, let yourself to relax and release whatever stress or tightness you may be carrying, surrendering to the present moment with an open heart and mind.

Love-Kindness Meditation

Loving-kindness meditation is a technique that encourages compassion and goodwill toward oneself and others. To practice loving-kindness meditation, choose a peaceful area to sit and close your eyes.

Begin by thinking of someone you care about, such as a family member, friend, or mentor. Silently repeat loving-kindness statements to this individual, such as *"May you be happy, healthy, safe, and at ease."* Allow yourself to truly connect with the goal behind each statement, sending feelings of love, caring, and compassion to yourself and others.

As you practice loving-kindness meditation, think about how it feels to create a sense of love and goodwill for yourself and people around you, and how it may change your connection with yourself and the world.

35

"When demands pull us in all ways, seeking refuge and repair is critical to our well-being. Enter yoga, a comprehensive practice that combines breath, movement, and mindfulness to promote harmony and balance in the body and mind."

CHAPTER 6

Yoga for Stress Relief: Nurturing Your Body and Spirit

Yoga is more than simply a physical activity; it is a comprehensive self-care regimen that includes the body, mind, and soul. Yoga, which is based on ancient Indian philosophy, tries to connect the individual self to the global consciousness by combining breath, movement, and meditation. Yoga is fundamentally a practice of self-inquiry and self-discovery, urging us to go into the depths of ourselves and awaken to our true nature.

Benefits of Yoga for Stress Relief

Yoga has several advantages for stress treatment, including physical, mental, and emotional well-being. Yoga relieves stress and stiffness in the body, improves flexibility and strength, and promotes relaxation and vitality.

Moving attentively and intentionally through a sequence of postures (asanas) allows us to release stored energy and restore balance to the body's energy centers (chakras), promoting harmony and well-being.

Mentally, yoga develops focus, attention, and awareness, helping us to calm our minds and discover serenity in the midst of commotion. We may increase our resistance to stresses and foster a sense of presence and calm by engaging in mindful movement and breath awareness.

Emotionally, yoga promotes self-compassion, acceptance, and appreciation, allowing us to deal with challenging emotions with grace and calm. Connecting with our deepest selves via yoga allows us to tap into a reservoir of strength, knowledge, and resilience that will carry us through life's problems with grace and ease.

Practical Techniques for Yoga Practice

To begin a yoga practice for stress alleviation, start slowly and carefully, respecting your body's limits and responding to its suggestions. Begin with a mild warm-up to awaken and prepare the body for movement, concentrating on deep, conscious breathing and easy stretches to relieve tension and tightness.

From there, you can go to a series of standing positions (such as mountain posture, warrior pose, and forward folds) to increase strength, stability, and balance while also developing attention and concentration.

As you progress through each position, pay attention to your body's feelings and the quality of your breath, allowing yourself to sink deeper into each posture with each exhale.

Remember to move deliberately and with intention, respecting your body's requirements and limitations while avoiding any motions or postures that create pain or suffering.

As your practice progresses, you can attempt more difficult postures and sequences while keeping a sense of awareness and present in your movement.

Restorative Yoga For Relaxation

Restorative yoga is a gentle, caring practice that focuses on relaxation and repair, making it one of the most effective types of yoga for stress treatment.

Restorative yoga positions are intended to put the body in profound relaxation, enabling the muscles to release tension and the mind to calm. Common restorative positions include supported child's pose, reclining bound angle pose, supported bridge pose, and legs-up-the-wall pose.

To perform restorative yoga, grab a few props like bolsters, blankets, and blocks and locate a quiet, comfortable place to practice. Begin with centering yourself and connecting with your breath, followed by a light warm-up to prepare the body for relaxation.

From there, continue on to a sequence of restorative postures, utilizing supports to help your body completely submit to each posture. Stay in each posture for a few minutes, concentrating on deep, conscious breathing and letting each exhale take you deeper into relaxation.

Mindful Meditation for Yoga Practice

In addition to physical positions, yoga makes mindfulness meditation a fundamental component of the practice. Mindful meditation in yoga entails paying attention to the breath and the body, noticing sensations as they come without judgment or attachment.

By building a feeling of presence and mindfulness in our practice, we may strengthen our connection to ourselves and the present moment, encouraging inner peace and serenity in the face of life's hardships.

Conclude with Savasana

Every yoga practice ends with savasana, the last relaxation posture, which serves as a moment for absorption and contemplation.

To perform savasana, lie on your back with your arms and legs gently wide apart and palms facing up. Close your eyes and let your body completely relax, releasing any tension or tightness with each exhalation. Stay in savasana for many minutes, letting yourself to completely submit to the present moment and reap the benefits of your practice.

Part III: Balance: Restoring Harmony in Your Life

"Genuine well-being begins with self-care, which is the discipline of feeding and sustaining oneself on all levels: mind, body, and spirit."

CHAPTER 7

Prioritizing Self-Care: Nourishing Your Mind, Body, and Soul

Self-care is more than just indulging ourselves with bubble baths and massages — it is a conscious and intentional practice of catering to our physical, emotional, and spiritual needs. From getting enough sleep and eating nutritious meals to participating in activities that offer us joy and fulfillment, self-care involves a wide variety of behaviors that promote our general well-being.

Self-care is about putting ourselves first and recognizing our own needs and limits, even in the middle of life's expectations and obligations.

The Value of Self-Care for Stress Relief

Prioritizing self-care is critical for managing stress and avoiding burnout. When we ignore our own needs and push ourselves beyond our limits, we become prone to physical, mental, and emotional tiredness, leaving us feeling exhausted and overwhelmed.

Making self-care a priority allows us to refill our energy stores, lessen the negative effects of stress on our health and well-being, and nurture greater resilience and vitality when faced with life's obstacles.

Practical Strategies for Self-Care

There are several methods to practice self-care; the goal is to choose what works best for you and include it into your daily routine. Here are some practical ways to prioritize self-care and nurture your mind, body, and soul:

1. Establish Healthy Routines: Begin by creating routines that promote your general well-being. This might involve establishing consistent sleep and waking hours, eating balanced meals at regular intervals, and engaging in regular physical activity. Prioritizing these fundamental self-care routines can help you build a solid foundation for general health and energy.

2. Establish Limits: Establish limits and say no to things that deplete energy or harm your well-being. It is OK to prioritize yourself and your own needs, even if it means disappointing others or missing out on chances. Remember that self-care is not selfish; it is necessary to sustain your health and happiness.

3. Prioritize Activities That offer You Joy: Schedule time for activities that offer you happiness, contentment, and relaxation. Whether it's spending time in nature, engaging in a hobby or creative outlet, or simply relaxing with a cup of tea and a good book, prioritize things that nourish your soul and boost your spirit.

4. Apply Mindfulness: Apply mindfulness and meditation into your everyday routine to reduce stress, cultivate presence, and promote serenity. Even a few minutes of focused breathing or meditation every day can significantly improve your mental and emotional well-being.

5. Connect with Others: Make time to connect with loved ones who encourage and support you. Social connection is vital for our mental well-being, and spending time with loved ones may provide us a feeling of belonging, support, and comfort during stressful times.

6. Seek Professional Support: If you're struggling to manage stress or prioritize self-care, it's important to seek help. Whether it's therapy, counseling, or coaching, seeking help may give vital insight and support on your path to wellness.

Cultivating Self-Compassion

Self-compassion is fundamental to self-care, which is the discipline of treating oneself with love, understanding, and acceptance, particularly during tough or painful situations. Rather of blaming ourselves for our perceived flaws or failings, self-compassion asks us to embrace ourselves with love and compassion, acknowledging that we are deserving of love and belonging just the way we are.

Self-compassion may help us modify our inner dialogue, create resilience in the face of hardship, and foster a strong feeling of self-worth and acceptance.

Overcoming Barriers to Self-Care

Despite its significance, prioritizing self-care can be difficult, particularly in a culture that values activity and production. Common obstacles to self-care include emotions of guilt or selfishness, fear of criticism or rejection, or just not knowing where to begin.

However, it's vital to remember that self-care isn't a luxury; it's an essential part of preserving our health and wellbeing. By identifying and resolving these obstacles with compassion and understanding, you can start prioritizing self-care and reap the rewards of a more balanced, meaningful existence.

"With efficient time management tactics, we can retake control of our calendars and make room for what is actually important."

CHAPTER 8

Time Management: Creating Space for What Matters

Time management is fundamentally the discipline of arranging and prioritizing tasks and activities in order to make the most use of your available time. It entails defining objectives, managing your calendar, and making deliberate decisions about how to spend your time and energy.

Effective time management is not about getting more done in less time, but about doing the right things at the right time and in the right way.

The Value of Time Management for Stress Relief

Effective time management is vital for lowering stress and avoiding burnout. When we feel overwhelmed by our obligations and commitments, we are more likely to get worried and nervous, which leads to lower productivity, poor performance, and a general lack of well-being.

By better organizing your time, you may lessen feelings of overwhelm, gain control, and make time for relaxation, rejuvenation, and self-care.

Practical Time Management Strategies

There are several time management tactics and approaches available; the key is to determine what works best for you and tailor it to your own requirements and preferences. Here are some practical time management methods to help you maximize your time and avoid stress:

1. Set Explicit Goals For Yourself: Both short-term and long-term. Having a clear vision of what you want to achieve can help you prioritize your chores and activities and stay focused on what's most important.

2. Prioritize Your Tasks: After setting goals, prioritize tasks and activities based on priority and urgency. To keep track of your projects and deadlines, use tools like to-do lists, calendars, and task management applications, and prioritize the most important activities first.

3. Break Down Large Projects Into Manageable Steps: To prevent procrastination and lost productivity. Break down enormous jobs into smaller, more manageable steps and do them one at a time. This will help you stay focused and motivated, making it simpler to achieve your goals.

4. Use Time Blocking: This time management strategy includes arranging certain blocks of time for various jobs and activities. By assigning allocated time for work, leisure, and self-care, you may build structure and rhythm in your day, minimize multitasking, and enhance productivity.

5. Use the Two-Minute Rule: This easy time management method will help you handle tiny activities and avoid them from building up. If a task takes less than two minutes, perform it right away rather than putting it off until later.

6. Minimize Distractions: Like social media, email, and noise to maintain attention and productivity. Set aside time for serious work, and utilize technologies like website blockers or noise-cancelling headphones to reduce distractions.

7. Take Regular Breaks To Relax And Refuel: Taking pauses can assist to avoid burnout, enhance attention and concentration, and boost overall productivity and well-being.

8. Review and Reflect: Conduct regular reviews of your objectives, priorities, and schedule to identify areas for improvement. Adjust your time management tactics as required to keep them aligned with your goals and well-being.

Overcoming Common Time Management Challenges

Despite our best efforts, we often find it difficult to manage our time properly. Procrastination, perfectionism, and trouble prioritizing activities are all examples of common time management issues.

However, by identifying and addressing these issues with compassion and understanding, you may devise solutions to overcome them while also strengthening your time management ability.

"Creating boundaries is critical for conserving energy, maintaining our well-being, and fostering successful relationships."

CHAPTER 9

Setting Boundaries: Protecting Your Energy and Well-being

Boundaries are the invisible lines that determine appropriate conduct and engagement in relationships. They serve as standards for how we expect to be treated by others and how we want to behave ourselves.

Healthy boundaries are critical for our physical, emotional, and mental well-being because they safeguard our energy, preserve our autonomy, and promote healthy relationships.

The Value of Boundaries for Well-Being

Setting limits is critical for maintaining our energy and wellbeing. Without clear limits, we may find ourselves overcommitted, overwhelmed, and exhausted, resulting in increased stress, anxiety, and burnout.

By setting and maintaining appropriate boundaries, we can make time for self-care, prioritize our own needs, and build more balance and harmony in our lives.

Types of Boundaries

Boundaries can take many shapes and relate to different aspects of our life. Some frequent types of borders are:

1. Physical Boundaries: These boundaries determine our physical space and privacy. They include personal space, physical touch, and limits for our items and goods.

2. Emotional Boundaries: Setting emotional boundaries protects us from being overwhelmed by others' feelings. They include things like expressing our emotions, limiting how much emotional assistance we can offer, and avoiding emotional manipulation or compulsion.

3. Mental barriers: These barriers shield our thoughts, beliefs, and views from being affected or undermined by others. They include honoring our intellectual autonomy, limiting the amount of information or input we let into our thoughts, and avoiding intellectual manipulation or gaslighting.

4. Time Boundaries: These boundaries help us manage our time and energy, preventing us from overcommitting or spreading ourselves too thin. They include limiting the amount of time we spend on work, social events, and personal hobbies, as well as prioritizing activities that are consistent with our beliefs and aspirations.

Practical Strategies for Setting Boundaries

Setting successful limits takes clarity, boldness, and self-awareness. Here are some practical ways for setting and keeping boundaries in several aspects of your life:

1. Determine Your Needs and Limitations: Begin by assessing your personal requirements, preferences, and limitations. What are your priorities? What makes you feel comfortable or uneasy? Understanding your personal boundaries allows you to convey them more successfully with others.

2. Set Boundaries Openly and Assertively: Use "I" phrases to convey your demands and preferences directly, rather than blaming or criticizing others. Be forceful and confident in your speech, and do not be hesitant to assert yourself.

3. Maintain Consistency: Establishing boundaries requires consistent behavior. Set a boundary and keep to it consistently, even if it is tough or painful. This provides a clear message to others about your expectations and helps to strengthen your limits over time.

4. Focus on Activities that Restore Energy: Make time for leisure, hobbies, and activities that offer you joy and fulfillment, and don't be afraid to say no to things that sap your energy or jeopardize your health.

Dealing with Common Boundary Challenges

Setting limits, even with our best intentions, can be difficult at times, especially when we are afraid of disagreement or rejection. Guilt, fear of confrontation, and concern about failing others are examples of common boundary problems.

However, by identifying and facing these problems head on, you then have in your hand the tactics for conquering them while expressing your limits with confidence and grace.

Part IV: Believe: Cultivating Resilience and Empowerment

"Our thinking determines our reality. Our perception of the environment, interpretation of events, and responses to difficulties all have a significant influence on our experiences and outcomes. Developing a positive mentality entails transitioning from limiting ideas to powerful thinking, as well as adopting optimism, resilience, and self-compassion."

CHAPTER 10

Cultivating a Positive Mindset: Shifting from Beliefs to Empowering Thoughts

Mindset refers to the ideas, attitudes, and assumptions that shape how we see ourselves, others, and the world around us. Our attitude influences our ideas, emotions, and behaviors, directing our activities and influencing our outcomes. There are two major types of mindsets: fixed mindsets and development mindsets.

Individuals with a fixed mindset feel that their abilities, intelligence, and talents are fixed and unchangeable. They may shun difficulties, dread failure, and see failures as proof of their shortcomings.

Individuals with a growth mindset, on the other hand, feel that their skills and talents may be honed through hard work, dedication, and study. They welcome challenges, see failure as an opportunity for progress, and are confident in their ability to learn and improve over time.

The Power of Positive Thinking

Positive thinking is the discipline of concentrating on the positive aspects of life, creating optimism, and viewing problems as chances for progress. According to research, having a positive mentality is related with various advantages, including:

1. *Improved Resilience:* A positive mentality cultivates resilience, allowing people to recover from failures, adapt to change, and endure in the face of adversity.

Positive thinking has been related to improved emotional well-being, lower stress levels, and enhanced happiness and life satisfaction.

2. *Better Health Outcomes:* Optimism has been linked to improved physical health outcomes, such as reduced rates of chronic illness, quicker recovery from sickness or accident, and longer life.

Practical Strategies for Developing a Positive Mindset

Cultivating a happy mentality is a lifetime process that involves deliberate effort and practice. Here are some practical techniques for establishing a happy attitude towards life:

1. Practice Gratitude: Think about what you're grateful for every day. Keeping a thankfulness diary, in which you write down three things you're grateful for every day, may help you focus on the good elements of your life and build a sense of appreciation and abundance.

2. Challenge Negative thinking: Identify and replace negative thinking with more powerful ones. Consider other explanations or interpretations that are more positive and empowering, as well as if there is evidence to back up the negative thought.

3. Surround Yourself With Good Influences: Such as supportive friends, inspirational literature, uplifting music, and motivating quotations. Seek out circumstances that promote happiness, and avoid events or people who deplete your energy or encourage negative views.

4. Practice Self-Compassion: Be nice and sympathetic to oneself, especially during difficult times or struggles. Treat yourself with the same warmth and understanding as you would a friend, and engage in self-care activities that promote your physical, emotional, and spiritual well-being.

5. Set Realistic Objectives: Set objectives that challenge and extend your talents, but are also attainable with hard work and perseverance. Break down huge ambitions into smaller, more doable tasks, and celebrate your accomplishments along the way.

6. Develop Optimism: Stay focused on what you can control and affect in your life, rather than obsessing on external factors. Maintain an optimistic attitude toward the future and believe in your abilities to overcome challenges and live the life you want.

7. See Failure As a Learning Opportunity: Consider failure to be a natural element of the learning process, as well as a chance for personal development. Instead than concentrating on previous mistakes or defeats, consider the lessons learned and how to apply them to future obstacles.

Defeating Negative Self-Talk

Negative self-talk is a typical impediment to developing a good attitude. It is the practice of criticizing or denigrating oneself, usually in reaction to challenges or perceived deficiencies.

To combat negative self-talk, work on self-awareness, challenging unpleasant beliefs, and replacing them with more positive and powerful affirmations.

"Building a support system entails surrounding yourself with people who care about you, understand you, and help you overcome life's obstacles."

CHAPTER 11

Building a Support System: Finding Strength in Community

A support system is a group of people who offer emotional, practical, and even financial assistance in times of need. Having individuals to lean on for support, whether they be family members, friends, coworkers, or members of a community or support group, may be important in navigating life's obstacles and enjoying its successes.

Benefits of a Support System

A robust support system provides several benefits to our mental, emotional, and physical well-being:

1. Emotional Support: A support system offers a secure environment in which to express feelings, communicate issues, and get validation and understanding from others. Knowing that we are not alone in our challenges can bring comfort and encouragement during tough times.

2. Practical Support: In addition to emotional support, a support system may provide practical assistance with activities such as childcare, housework, transportation, and financial aid as needed.

3. Social Connection: Connecting with people through a support system promotes a sense of belonging, connection, and social support, all of which are critical for our mental and emotional well.

4. Enhanced Resilience: Having a support system can help us be more resilient and manage with stress, hardship, and life's obstacles. Knowing that we have individuals who love and support us might give us the strength and confidence to tackle challenging situations.

Cultivating Supportive Relationships

Creating a support system involves deliberate work and cultivating relationships with people. Here are some practical ways for creating helpful connections and building a solid support system:

1. Identify Your help Network: Identify those in your life who can provide you with help, such as family, friends, coworkers, or community/support groups. Consider who you feel comfortable confiding in and who you can rely on for help when you need it.

2. Communicate Your wants: Be transparent with your support network about your wants and worries. Tell them how they can best help you, whether it's by lending a listening ear, providing practical aid, or simply being there for you during difficult times.

3. Be a Supportive Friend: To create a strong support system, it's necessary to provide and receive support. Be a good listener, express empathy and affirmation, and give practical aid as required. Create genuine connections with people via mutual trust, respect, and support.

4. Joining Support Organizations: Consider joining support organizations or communities based on your hobbies, principles, or unique needs. Connecting with others who share similar experiences, whether in the form of a support group for people dealing with a specific health condition, a community organization focused on a shared hobby or interest, or an online forum for discussing mental health, can provide valuable support and understanding.

Developing a support system can be difficult at times, especially if you suffer from social anxiety, trust difficulties, or a lack of social support.

However, it is critical to acknowledge that everyone deserves assistance and to take proactive actions to overcome obstacles to developing a support system. This might include obtaining help from a therapist or counselor, gradually increasing your social network, or looking into other sources of support like online groups or helplines.

"Embracing change entails developing flexibility, resilience, and adaptability in order to manage transitions gracefully and confidently."

CHAPTER 12

Embracing Change: Thriving Through Life's Transitions

Change is an essential part of the human experience. It refers to both exterior changes in our surroundings and interior changes in our attitudes, beliefs, and emotions. Change may be frightening and disruptive, but it also provides opportunity for development, learning, and transformation.

By accepting change as a natural and unavoidable aspect of life, we create an open and curious mentality that helps us to handle changes more easily and confidently.

The Effect of Change on Our Lives

Change may have a significant influence on our lives, eliciting a wide range of feelings such as exhilaration, anxiety, grief, and uncertainty. Major life transitions, such as beginning a new job, quitting a relationship, or losing a loved one, can rock our foundation and test our sense of identity, purpose, and belonging.

Even little changes, like as relocating to a new place or beginning a new pastime, can upset our habits and necessitate adjustments. However, change provides possibilities for personal development, self-discovery, and fresh starts.

Practical Strategies for Accepting Change

While change might be unpleasant, there are practical ways for embracing it and navigating transitions with grace and perseverance. Here are some tips to help you embrace change and flourish during life transitions:

1. Develop Resilience: Resilience is the capacity to overcome failures, adapt to change, and flourish in the face of adversity. Cultivate resilience by practicing coping skills like mindfulness, self-compassion, and problem-solving, as well as viewing obstacles as opportunities for growth and learning.

2. Practice Acceptance: Accepting change as a normal element of life. Instead of opposing or denying change, practice acceptance by allowing yourself to feel the whole spectrum of emotions that come with it, and believing in your capacity to handle change with grace and bravery.

3. Maintain Perspective: Remind yourself that change is transient and you have the power and resources to overcome problems and adjust to new situations. Emphasize the benefits of change, such as possibilities for development, learning, and personal transformation.

4. Be Flexible: Flexibility is adapting to changing conditions and adjusting plans and expectations accordingly. Stay flexible by keeping open to new options and solutions, as well as being willing to let go of old habits, beliefs, and routines that are no longer serving you.

5. Seek Support: In times of transition, it's crucial to seek help from friends, family, or a support network. Reach out to people for emotional support, encouragement, and advice, and don't be afraid to ask for assistance when you need it. Creating a strong support network may give a sense of belonging, validation, and reassurance during times of transition.

6. Set Objectives: Set objectives that correspond with your beliefs, interests, and aspirations. Take action to achieve them. Setting goals may give direction and purpose during times of change, and taking modest, achievable actions toward those objectives can help you reclaim control and agency in your life.

7. Embrace Uncertainty: Uncertainty is a normal component of change, and learning to embrace it may help you negotiate transitions with comfort and confidence. Instead of being afraid of the unknown, approach it with curiosity and openness, knowing that you are resilient and resourceful enough to deal with anything comes your way.

Change, despite its promise for development and transformation, is not always welcomed. Fear of the unknown, connection to the familiar, and a need for control are all common impediments to accepting change.

However, by noticing and resolving these barriers with compassion and self-awareness, you create an open and flexible attitude that helps you to welcome change more easily and confidently.

Part V: Integration and Transformation

"By creating a personalized plan that incorporates numerous approaches and practices, you will successfully manage stress, foster mental resilience, and boost physical vigor, resulting in a more balanced and meaningful existence."

CHAPTER 13

Creating Your Personal Blueprint for Stress, Mind Reset, and Body Rejuvenation

Before you begin designing your unique blueprint, you should consider your specific requirements, interests, and priorities. Take some time to ponder on:

1. Your Stress Triggers: Determine which circumstances or situations in your life cause stress, such as work-related demands, relationship troubles, financial concerns, or health issues.

2. Your Coping Strategies: Consider the coping skills you presently employ to deal with stress, such as exercise, meditation, creative outlets, social support, and relaxation techniques.

3. Your Health Goals: Clarify your health objectives and aspirations, whether they be to improve physical fitness, increase mental clarity, reduce anxiety, improve sleep quality, or nurture stronger emotional resilience.

Gaining clarity on these factors will allow you to design your own plan to successfully handle your specific demands and situations.

Components of Your Personal Blueprint

Your unique blueprint for stress reduction, mind reset, and body rejuvenation may include a variety of approaches and activities that enhance overall well-being. Here are some crucial components to consider include in your plan:

1. **Stress Management Techniques:** As discussed in the previous chapters, learn stress management skills to reduce tension and enhance relaxation. This might include:

A. Mindfulness Meditation: Practice mindfulness meditation to cultivate present-moment awareness, reduce stress, and enhance mental clarity.

B. Deep Breathing Exercises: Integrate deep breathing exercises into your daily routine to calm the nervous system, reduce anxiety, and promote relaxation.

C. Progressive Muscle Relaxation: Learn progressive muscle relaxation techniques to release tension and promote physical and mental relaxation.

2. Mind Reset Practices: Establish behaviors that promote mental clarity, attention, and emotional resilience. Consider incorporating:

A. Journaling: Begin a journaling practice to reflect on your ideas, feelings, and experiences while also gaining insight into your thinking and behavior patterns.

B. Visualization: Use visualization techniques to envisage good possibilities, set objectives, and develop a sense of confidence and empowerment.

C. Gratitude Practice: Develop a daily gratitude practice to focus on the good things in your life and cultivate a sense of thankfulness and happiness.

3. Body Rejuvenation Strategies: Take proactive efforts to improve your physical health, energy, and general well-being. This may involve:

A. *Regular Exercise:* Regular physical exercise promotes cardiovascular health, improves mood, reduces stress, and increases overall fitness levels.

B. *Healthy Nutrition:* To promote maximum health and vitality, eat a balanced and nutritious diet rich in whole foods, fruits, vegetables, lean meats, and healthy fats.

C. *Quality Sleep:* Prioritize excellent sleep by sticking to a consistent sleep schedule, developing a calming bedtime ritual, and creating a sleep-friendly atmosphere that promotes restorative sleep.

4. Self-Care Practices: Integrate self-care routines into your daily routine to promote physical, emotional, and mental well. This might include:

A. *Mindful Movement:* Use mindful movement techniques like yoga, tai chi, or qigong to increase flexibility, strength, and relaxation.

B. Pampering Rituals: To relax and revitalize, indulge in frequent pampering rituals such as hot baths, massages, and spa treatments.

C. Digital Detox: Take regular breaks from digital gadgets and screens to decrease stress, improve sleep quality, and boost general health.

Creating Your Action Plan

Once you've defined the components of your personal blueprint, it's time to develop a detailed action plan for execution. Consider the steps below:

1. Set Clear Goals: Set clear, quantifiable objectives for each component of your plan, such as regular meditation, exercise, or journaling.

2. Establish Daily Habits: Create daily habits that align with your goals, such as meditation, exercise, and thankfulness.

3. Create a Schedule: Plan a weekly calendar to give time to each component of your design, providing balance and consistency in your practice.

4. Monitor Progress: Regularly track your progress, identify issues, and alter your strategy accordingly.

5. Be Flexible and Adaptive: Adjust your approach to life's unforeseen obstacles and changes.

Throughout the process of implementing your personal blueprint, practice mindfulness and introspection to increase your awareness of your thoughts, emotions, and experiences. Take time to consider the impact of your practices, noticing any changes in your stress, mood, energy, or overall well-being. Celebrate your accomplishments, and be compassionate with yourself when facing a struggle or setback.

"Going on a path to well-being is more than just making momentary adjustments; it's about building long-term habits and practices that promote health and pleasure."

CHAPTER14

Sustaining Your Journey: Strategies for Long-Term Well-being

Maintaining your well-being journey necessitates a willingness to embrace lifestyle changes that promote your physical, mental, and emotional health. Here are some important methods to consider:

1. Pay Attention to Yourself: Set aside time each day to indulge in things that feed your mind, body, and soul, such as meditation, exercise, nature walks, or hobbies that you like.

2. Foster Healthy Relationships: Build supportive relationships with friends, family, and community people who inspire and motivate you. Surround yourself with people who share your beliefs, interests, and goals, and who inspire you to be your best.

3. Practice Mindful Eating: Pay attention to your body's hunger and fullness cues, consume entire, nutrient-dense meals, and enjoy each mouthful. Avoid restrictive diets and instead adopt a balanced approach to nutrition that meets your body's demands.

4. Effective Stress Management: Develop healthy coping techniques including deep breathing, meditation, exercise, and spending time in nature. Prioritize stress management tactics that appeal to you and apply them into your daily routine to boost resilience and well-being.

Cultivating Resilience And Adaptability

Life is full of ups and downs, and maintaining your well-being path necessitates perseverance and adaptation in the face of obstacles and disappointments. Here are some ways for developing resilience and adaptability:

1. Embrace Flexibility: Be open to change and recognize life's uncertain nature. Accept uncertainty as a chance for development and learning, and adjust your plans and objectives as necessary to reflect your changing needs and priorities.

2. Learn from Setbacks: View setbacks and obstacles as chances to learn and improve. Instead of concentrating on previous mistakes or failures, consider the lessons they teach and how you might utilize them to guide your future actions and decisions.

Cultivating Gratitude and Positivity

Practicing appreciation and keeping a happy mentality are critical for maintaining your well-being journey throughout time. Here are some techniques to cultivate thankfulness and positivity:

1. Begin a Gratitude Journal: Write down three things you're grateful for every day. Cultivate a grateful attitude by concentrating on the good things in your life and expressing thanks for your blessings.

2. Surround Yourself with Positivity: Surround oneself with good influences, such as helpful friends, inspiring literature, uplifting music, and encouraging phrases. Seek out circumstances that promote happiness, and avoid events or people who deplete your energy or encourage negative views.

3. Practice Positive Affirmations: Use positive affirmations to overcome negative self-talk and build a positive view on life. Repeat affirmations like "I am capable," "I am worthy," and "I am resilient" to reinforce your positive self-image and talents.

Reflecting and Adjusting Your Approach

Finally, maintaining your well-being journey necessitates continuous reflection and change to your approach. Take regular breaks to reflect on your progress, appreciate your accomplishments, and discover areas for development. Be willing to alter your objectives, routines, and methods as required to keep up with your changing requirements and priorities.

CONCLUSION

Embracing Your Radiant, Resilient Self

As you reach the final pages of *"***Breath, Balance, Believe:** A Woman's Blueprint for Stress Relief, Mind Reset, and Body Rejuvenation,"* I trust you've found within its wisdom a guiding light for your journey ahead.

In these pages, you've uncovered the potency of your breath to ground you in the present moment, the significance of maintaining balance in nurturing your overall well-being, and the unwavering belief in your innate power to shape your own destiny. Through the melding of ancient teachings and modern insights, you've mapped out a path toward greater vitality, clarity, and joy.

As you close this chapter, know that it marks not the end, but rather, a new beginning—a chapter brimming with endless opportunities, boundless potential, and the radiant, resilient self that resides within you. May the wisdom gleaned from these teachings continue to guide and inspire you as you navigate the ebb and flow of life's journey.

In reflection, I urge you to honor yourself—for the courage you've shown, the growth you've experienced, and the unshakeable belief you've cultivated in your own ability to thrive. May your path toward stress relief, mind reset, and body rejuvenation be filled with moments of joy, fulfillment, and an unwavering sense of confidence in the remarkable woman you are.

About The Author

Elsie James is a renowned author who has made a significant impact in the fields of both parenting and women's empowerment. With a focus on offering insightful and practical advice, Elsie has penned three remarkable books, *"Dealing with Separation Anxiety in Children: Practical Tips for Parents"*, *"Coping with Divorce: Tips for Helping Children Navigate a Difficult Time"* and *"Overcoming Parenting Burnout: Tips For Recharging And Reconnecting With Your Family"* which provide invaluable guidance and support for parents facing the challenges of raising children.

In addition to her contributions to parenting literature, Elsie has also delved into the realm of women's well-being with her latest book, *"Breath, Balance, Believe: A Woman's Blueprint for Stress Relief, Mind Reset, and Body Rejuvenation."* This exciting work offers women valuable insights, strategies, and personal anecdotes to help them navigate life's demands with grace and resilience.

Elsie's expertise and compassionate approach have established her as a respected authority in both parenting and women's literature. Her books continue to inspire and empower readers worldwide, offering them the tools they need to navigate the complexities of parenting and womanhood with confidence, love, and a renewed sense of purpose.